Forced March

Miklós Radnóti

Forced March
Selected Poems

Translated from the Hungarian
by
Clive Wilmer and George Gömöri

ENITHARMON PRESS

ejps

in association with
The European Jewish Publication Society

First published in 2003
by the Enitharmon Press
26B Caversham Road
London NW5 2DU

www.enitharmon.co.uk

in association with
The European Jewish Publication Society
PO Box 19948
London N3 3ZL

www.ejps.org.uk

Reprinted 2010

*The European Jewish Publication Society is a registered charity which gives grants to assist
in the publication and distribution of books relevant to Jewish literature, history, religion,
philosophy, politics and culture.*

Distributed in the UK by
Central Books
99 Wallis Road
London E9 5LN

ISBN 978 1 900564 53 3

British Library Cataloguing-in-Publication Data.
A catalogue record for this book is available
from the British Library.

Typeset in Caslon by Servis Filmsetting Ltd

Printed and bound in Great Britain by
CPI Antony Rowe, Chippenham and Eastbourne

ACKNOWLEDGEMENTS

Enitharmon Press gratefully acknowledges the financial support of
Arts Council England (London), The European Jewish Publication
Society, the Hungarian Cultural Centre (with the general support of
the Hungarian Ministry of Cultural Heritage) and the Translation
Fund of the Hungarian Book Foundation.

MINISTRY OF CULTURAL HERITAGE

Contents

Miklós Radnóti © Petőfi Literary Museum, Budapest

PREFACE TO THE REVISED EDITION (2003)

It is more than thirty years since we first translated a poem by Miklós Radnóti. Some time later, in 1979, the first edition of *Forced March* appeared, published by Carcanet Press. By the mid-1980s, that edition had sold out. Before 1979, there had been three English selections of Radnóti, two of them issued by American publishers, the third by a very small British one. Since our book there have been six more, one of them *The Complete Poetry*, four hundred pages of it, translated by Emery George. Translations of Radnóti, including several of ours, have appeared in many anthologies, especially collections of Second World War or so-called Holocaust poetry. Three major studies of Radnóti's work – by Marianna D. Birnbaum, Emery George and Zsuzsanna Ozsváth – have been published, as have the papers of a Radnóti memorial conference edited by ourselves. (The conference was held at Darwin College, Cambridge, in 1994.) Radnóti has also become a name in English literature, featuring in a novel by the late Wilbur Sanders *Like the Big Wolves*, in *The Radnóti Poems* by John Kinsella and in an exceptionally beautiful passage from Geoffrey Hill's *The Triumph of Love*.

It was clear in this context that we could not simply reprint the first edition of *Forced March*. Not only was Radnóti now a figure in the landscape, but our own view of him had developed, as had our skills as poets and translators. We therefore decided to revise the poems and to add some new versions. It is in the nature of the translation process that poems that once seemed untranslatable can come in time to seem quite the opposite. This has meant that versions we were never entirely content with have now been substantially revised – a good example would be 'Neither Memory, nor Magic' – and others which eluded us altogether in the 1970s have now been turned into English without too much anguish. (The wholly new versions are 'Song of Death', 'In the Margins of the Prophet

11

Habakkuk', 'In a Restless Hour', 'Written in a Copy of *Steep Path*', 'Skin and Bone and Pain', 'The Terrible Angel', 'Paris' and 'Oh Ancient Prisons'.) It is perhaps a sign of the times, and an encouraging one, that in 1979 we thought 'cultural' translation was sometimes necessary – that the English reader could not cope with (for instance) common Hungarian names. We have abandoned that preconception and made up for it by amplifying the notes.

Radnóti has acquired many English-speaking readers in the past thirty years or so. It is our conviction that so marvellous and universal a poet can win a great many more.

George Gömöri
Clive Wilmer

INTRODUCTION

On 9 November 1944, Miklós Radnóti was executed by firing-squad. He was 35. He had been encamped in Serbia, attached to a forced labour battalion under German command, but as the Axis armies began their retreat from the Eastern front, they drove the labourers westward across Hungary. Near the village of Abda in the north-west, those who were too weak to continue the march into Germany were shot by their guards and buried in a mass grave. When the bodies were exhumed the following year, a notebook full of poems – some written within days of his death – was found in Radnóti's greatcoat. They are formal poems of classical precision: poems which, though overshadowed by the horrors of war and the poet's certainty of a premature death, are committed to the most humane values our civilisation has nurtured. The formality and precision are themselves manifestations of those values and, as such, declarations of the poet's commitment. For nearly ten years he had been preparing himself for such a death. To read his work chronologically is to follow something of the process whereby an individual talent is moulded by historical events; at the same time, it is to perceive that talent discerning meaning in the events, even as it is transformed by them.

Radnóti was born in Budapest in 1909. Of Jewish origin, he seems to have felt no special attachment to his race or religion, though it is arguable that Judaism was to exercise an influence on his poetry. From the outset his life was marked by insecurity. His mother died giving birth to him and his father died soon afterwards. The wealthy uncle who adopted him was generous and bought him a good education, but the poet's feelings toward him were never other than ambivalent.

His insecurity was exacerbated by the troubled political climate of the *entre-deux-guerres* period. Between 1920 and 1944, Hungary was governed by Admiral Horthy and his pseudo-parliamentary regime. Horthy was an ultra-conservative nationalist, a cautious authoritarian who attempted to stifle all opposition or protest. His policies, aimed at regaining ethnic Hungarian territories lost at the end of the First World War, were ultimately to throw his country into the arms of Hitler. To Radnóti, as a libertarian Socialist and an idealistic man of letters, such a government was hard to endure, though it was not until 1938 that anti-Jewish legislation featured in the government's 'reform programme'.

By 1934, when he graduated from Szeged University with a distinction in Hungarian and French, Radnóti already had three books of poetry to his credit. The main influences on the early verse are predictable: the French *avant-garde*, German Expressionism and a Hungarian version of Constructivism associated with the Socialist poet and theoretician Lajos Kassák. Radnóti's first book, *Pagan Invocation* (1930), consists mainly of dithyrambic, Whitmanesque celebrations of life, nature and erotic love, though the mature poet is already in evidence in the more muted passages with their warmth and melancholy and certain gestures towards Christian symbolism. Around 1932, the vague, undirected rebelliousness he shared with so many of his contemporaries began to take on a more concrete form: political protest started to figure in his poems. At this stage he was still thinking and writing in categories of a somewhat nebulous Marxism. But he resisted orthodoxy. He was soon to become a close admirer of Sándor Sík, a Catholic poet-priest who taught at Szeged and whose influence on him was to prove profound and lasting. Before long the 'proletarian poet' stance had given way to a deeper concern with political developments at home and abroad. His work was gradually becoming a sort of political seismograph: it could register the slightest tremor in advance of an earthquake.

Radnóti's response to the rise of Hitler was almost immediate. In a love poem dated September 1934 he wrote – with an obvious allusion to Nazi terror –

> You embrace her to protect her, while around you
> The world lies in wait for you
> To kill you finally with its long knives.

From now on, Radnóti saw himself as a doomed man. The danger of similar developments in Hungary was not yet so great, but he was quick to respond to the effects of Fascism elsewhere. All over Europe, it seemed to him, the enemy was closing in, and his sense of a malign personal fate was soon bound up with his sympathy for those already suffering. His fifth book, published in the first year of the Spanish Civil War, bears the title *Keep Walking, You, the Death-Condemned* (1936). He had solved the problem. The question was no longer 'Shall I die?' or 'May I die?' in the coming war, but '*How* shall I die?' 'And as for you, young man, what mode of death awaits you?' he asks in the poem that opens the present selection. For the eight years that remained to him, this *modus moriendi* was to be his central concern.

This calm contemplation of violent death, which recurs throughout Radnóti's mature work, is remorseless almost to the point of morbid obsession. What exactly is to account for it? Hungarian critics with a psychoanalytical bias have pointed to a latent guilt-complex: the knowledge that his own birth had caused his mother's death, the theory goes, filled Radnóti with the urge to atone, to offer himself as an expiating sacrifice. There is evidence of such an anxiety in some of the poems – for example the 'Fourth Eclogue' and 'The Terrible Angel' – but as an explanation it is inadequate. There is little in the poems that could be ascribed to a death-wish, nor any sense that he actually courted the fate he was only too justified in predicting for himself. The truth is rather that his work is steeped in an awareness of death. This awareness, based on presentiment, was rationally sustained by a variety of preoccupations: his Jewish origin, his developing interest in the Christian concept of sacrifice (he was received into the Roman Catholic Church during the war) and his concern that European humanism might fall to Nazi barbarism.

This is where Lorca appears as a figure of great symbolic importance. Since the publication of Ian Gibson's *The Death of Lorca* (1973), there has been little reason to doubt what Radnóti assumed when news of the poet's 'execution' reached him: like others who sympathised with the Spanish Republican cause, he took it that Lorca had been murdered by the Nationalists. If this was so, it was also clear that he had not been killed – as Radnóti might himself have expected to be – on grounds of race or revolutionary belief. In Radnóti's interpretation, Lorca *had* to die: because he was loved by the people and because, quite simply, he was a poet, a spokesman for the forces of life. Behind his death there lay a simple equation: Fascism equals war equals death. It kills poets merely for being poets.

Once Radnóti had accepted this eventuality and seen it as part of his destiny, his whole sense of the physical world changed. Gone were the idyllic landscapes of *Pagan Invocation*. He began to read omens in the clouds, to hear strange squeals and whimpers in the hushed garden, to watch the splendours of autumn with the eyes of a man to whom little of life remains. The generalised formulas of Expressionist imagery become sharper and more specific. They are more individually registered and with greater urgency. Joy and anxiety seem to become as tangible as the images that evoke them. For joy is as present as anxiety. Though fearful of the future, Radnóti enjoyed domestic happiness: in 1935 he had married Fanni Gyarmati, whose love was to sustain him through the suffering of the years to come, and whose constancy again and again redeems the world of the last poems from the chaos which has otherwise usurped it.

As the Second World War approached, Hungary drifted slowly but surely into the Axis alliance. The historian C. A. Macartney has written that, between 1937 and 1944, Hungarian internal politics were 'little more than a function of foreign politics, and the history of Hungary during the same years is little more than that of her relations with Germany'. Radnóti's fears began to prove justified when, in 1938 and again in 1939, the Hungarian government began to legislate against the Jews. In 1941 it granted the Germans permission to cross its territory and invade Yugoslavia, part of which was then annexed by Hungary. In the same year, it declared war on the Soviet Union, thus openly committing itself to the Axis. Eventually, in March 1944, the Germans occupied Hungary and the German ambassador nominated the government.

In the course of these events, the fate Radnóti had so long foreseen was gradually fulfilled. From 1940 onwards, he was conscripted for service in various forced labour battalions. Shortly after the Nazi takeover in Budapest, he was sent to the German-controlled copper-mines at Bor in Serbia. There he worked on the construction of a railway-line between Bor and Belgrade. There, too, he wrote many of his finest poems: 'Letter to My Wife', 'A la Recherche', 'Root' and the last two of the cycle of Eclogues. It was when the prison-camp at Bor was evacuated in the autumn of 1944 that he and his fellow-labourers began the forced march that was to culminate in his death.

The Radnóti of the late poems is basically a Christian Stoic. As such, he now saw his own survival as of secondary importance: he had been called 'As witness to the truth'. In the last decade of his life he seems to have been striving for what his contemporary Attila József called 'diamond consciousness': to focus all his spiritual and intellectual resources into one powerful beam of poetic energy. There is evidence in the poems of a growing preoccupation with the body/soul dichotomy and speculation about the ways of the soul after bodily death. The whole structure of his vision was now fundamentally Judaeo-Christian, with Socialism as the secular complement to his religion. When the Prophet Nahum in the 'Eighth Eclogue' invites the Poet to join him in preaching 'the Kingdom about to be born', he is clearly referring to the Kingdom of God as promised by Jesus. Yet the phrase should also be read politically and historically. Thus, the poem not only dramatises the continuity of the Jewish and Christian revelations; it also locates the roots of millenarian Socialism in the same tradition. Nor do the reconciliations stop there. The role of the prophet in the ancient world is equated with that of the poet in the modern; and the language and teaching of the Bible are set in a poetic form whose origins are pagan and classical. The poem brings together in this way the different strands of the humanist culture whose future had seemed so severely threatened. But the emphasis has changed. In the late 1930s it had seemed inevitable that poets would 'disappear' as strangely as Lorca had – with maybe a few fragments of their work surviving for 'the curious who come after us'. In 1944, as Radnóti moved towards his death, to bear witness to the truth in verse had become much more than a gesture of defiance or self-defence. It had become a way of identifying himself with the values under threat and, thus, of sustaining them.

17

Commitment to such values involved commitment to the forms and language associated with them. By the mid-1930s, Radnóti's aim was no longer to provoke admiration or opposition; his purpose now was to express certain moods and formulate certain ideas as clearly and exactly as possible. This involved a return to rhyme, regular stanzas and traditional metres. Although he remained spiritually attached to Romantic hopes and ideals, the forms through which he communicated were increasingly classical. This retreat to classical metres and a vocabulary associated with translations of Virgil and Horace was more than a gesture towards a dying tradition. For a man writing at the very edge of survival, whose finest work flowered in conditions of intellectual darkness and moral anarchy, the expression of thought and feeling within the clear but flexible order of the Latin hexameter came to seem a moral act. And it constituted a defensive bulwark against the uncertainty of the world.

Radnóti's commitment to truth and form was – quite literally – ultimate. His 'Postcards', more or less scribbled on the march, are brief messages from Purgatory. They are unflinchingly realistic in their delineation of the horrors of war, yet never lose sight of the possibility of a better life. Against a background of villages on fire, he glimpses 'a tiny shepherdess' still going about her ordinary life and yet, in that setting, evoking the fragility of a porcelain figurine. Then finally, a few days before the end, he anticipates the manner of his going with uncanny precision:

> Shot in the neck. 'This is how you will end,'
> I whispered to myself. 'Keep lying still.
> Now, patience is flowering into death.'

The present selection is confined to poems from Radnóti's last three books: *Keep Walking, You, the Death-Condemned* (1936), *Steep Path* (1938) and the posthumous *Foaming Sky* (1946). In other words, we have aimed at providing an introduction to the mature poetry in preference to a general view of Radnóti's development. He has often been referred to as a 'labour-camp' or 'anti-Fascist' poet, as if such phrases were sufficient to define his achievement. It is certainly relevant to an understanding of these poems to know that they tell the truth from experience about that most inconceivable phase of our history. What is still more relevant is the fact that the author was able to make great poems out of the experience, and that the courage their writing demanded was an essential feature of his creative impulse. The measure of Radnóti's achievement is that he remained articulate about the horrors of his time and transmuted them into poems that reach to beauty and serenity. In the end, as his friend the poet István Vas suggested, the moral and artistic perfection of Radnóti's work, the truth of it and its beauty, are inseparable. His poems are, said Vas, 'among the rare masterpieces that combine artistic and moral perfection . . . not just an exciting body of work, not just truly great poems, but also an example of human and artistic integrity that is as embarrassing and absurd as it is imperative'.

George Gömöri
Clive Wilmer

A NOTE ON THE TRANSLATION

This book began life as a series of literal translations by George Gömöri from his native language. My task was to turn his tentative, lineated prose into something that could be read without discomfort as English verse. Having done so, I would then present him with the results and together we would work to bring the finished product as close to the Hungarian as we could – without losing its qualities as readable English verse. The poems are in no sense 'imitations' or free variations, though we have regarded form and content as of about equal importance and, where they proved incompatible, allowed ourselves minor liberties.

The emphasis on form may at first sound surprising. From the outset we agreed that Radnóti's adoption of certain fixed forms, especially those derived from classical authors, was inseparable from his 'message'. It would be impossible to convey the full weight of his Eclogues, for example, in free verse. As it happens, the Latin hexameter has a clear equivalent in Hungarian verse, one almost as familiar to the Hungarian ear as the iambic pentameter is to ours. One of my most difficult tasks was to find an English measure as flexible as the pentameter, yet long enough to render the 'packed' feeling of the Virgilian line. In English, unlike Hungarian, the quantitative metres of Latin are impossible, and a line over five feet long runs the risk of monotony. In the end, I opted for an English line of six accents, which owes something to the longer line as used by Thomas Hardy. (With his feeling for his native country and his love of the classical pastoral, Hardy often provided a useful model, a sort of English analogy for Radnóti.)

The rhymed verse presented different problems. There are two metrical systems available to the Hungarian lyric poet. One is the quantitative system, which Radnóti uses in the Horatian lyric 'In a Restless Hour'. More often than not, though, poets use a native

Hungarian system based on syllabic clusters. The former can be roughly imitated by substituting accents for long syllables. The latter, though, has no equivalent; one can write in lines of similar length but otherwise the conventions used will be English. I found it best, in these circumstances, to make different decisions for different poems. The title-poem, 'Forced March', is written in a regular form based on Walther von der Vogelweide's 'Owê war sint verswunden · alliu mîniu jâr'. Radnóti in effect alludes to the German poem, but the form is there for metrical as well as thematic effect: its rhythm mimes the monotony and foot-slogging fatigue of the march. An exact reproduction of the metre in English would have caught the monotony but little else, so I opted for a less strident paradigm: a line of six accents, divided by the caesura into equal hemistiches, but disregarding the number of syllables. In several other poems Radnóti uses a similar metre, though usually with significant variations: the 'Second Eclogue', 'I Cannot Tell', 'Neither Memory, nor Magic', 'Your Right Hand under My Neck' and 'Just as Unnoticed'. In most of these I simply adopted my version of the hexameter. In one or two of them, I varied the line-length slightly from time to time. In the case of 'Night', which is in hexameter couplets in the original, my usual line seemed too cumbersome, so I settled for unrhymed English syllabics. The stanzaic poems were easier to imitate, though often I was obliged to replace a full Hungarian rhyme (usually disyllabic) with the most tenuous of English half-rhymes.

The use of rhyme in verse translation inevitably entails periphrasis, jugglings with word-order and, occasionally, the addition of a word or phrase. Sometimes such exigencies served to clarify the English sense, especially in the austerer poems where the feeling in the Hungarian was a matter of rhythm or association. For example, in 'Foaming Sky', I added the word 'appalled' to the second stanza, partly for the sake of a rhyme and partly to focus the feeling.

Finally, there is the matter of diction. Radnóti draws on a wide range of influences, most of which affect his choice of words. French poetry from the Renaissance on contributed to his ideal of clarity. Modern German poetry is behind the Expressionistic quality of certain images. But much the most important of his sources were the Bible and the Classics. In the last months of his life, Radnóti seems to have had no general access to books, but he carried about with him a slightly modernised version of the book he valued above all others: the Hungarian Bible of 1590, translated by the Calvinist Gáspár Károli. Analogy with the King James seemed apposite, so I often consulted it for a word or a turn of phrase. (This is especially true of the heavily allusive 'Eighth Eclogue'.) I have also – as Radnóti himself did – made use of locutions associated with classical translation.

The diction of these poems is often artificial, though the artifice is sometimes undermined by irony. The diction, like the forms, was intended to carry significant moral weight.

Clive Wilmer

Long the gods, we know,
Have grudged thee, Caesar, to the world below,
*Where fraud and rapine right and wrong confound,**
Where impious arms from every part resound,
And monstrous crimes in every shape are crowned.
The peaceful peasant to the wars is pressed;
The fields lie fallow in inglorious rest;
The plain no pasture to the flock affords;
The crooked scythes are straightened into swords:
And there Euphrates her soft offspring arms,
And here the Rhine rebellows with alarms;
The neighbouring cities range on several sides,
Perfidious Mars long-plighted leagues divides,
And o'er the wasted world in triumph rides.
So four fierce coursers, starting to the race,
Scour through the plain, and lengthen every pace;
Nor reins, nor curbs, nor threatening cries, they fear,
But force along the trembling charioteer.

Virgil, *The Georgics*
(translated by John Dryden)

GARDEN ON ISTENHEGY

Summer has fallen asleep, it drones, and a grey veil
  Is drawn across the bright face of the day;
  A shadow vaults a bush, so my dog growls,
  His hackles bristling, then he runs away.

Shedding its petals one by one, a late flower stands
  Naked and half-alive. I hear the sound
  Of a withered apricot-bough crack overhead
  To sink of its own weight slowly to the ground.

Oh and the garden too prepares for sleep, its fruit
  Proffered to the heavy season of the dead.
  It is getting dark. Late too, a golden bee
  Is flying a death-circle around my head.

And as for you, young man, what mode of death awaits you?
  Will a shot hum like a beetle toward your heart,
  Or a loud bomb rend the earth so that your body
  Falls limb from limb, your young flesh torn apart?

In sleep the garden breathes. I question it in vain.
  Though still unanswered, I repeat it all.
  The noonday sun still flows in the ripe fruit
  Touched by the twilight chill of the dew fall.

20 July 1936

KEEP WALKING, YOU, THE DEATH-CONDEMNED

Keep walking, you, the death-condemned!
In front, the dark trees ranged in line
Topple towards you; bushes hide
A cat and the chill wind. The road
Turns white with fear, arching its spine.

Shrivel away now, autumn leaves!
Shrivel, oh terrifying world!
Cold hissing from the sky is harsh,
And on stiff, rusty blades of grass
The shadows of wild ducks are hurled.

Oh poet, now live a pure life –
As dwellers on the snow-capped, tall
Mountains the wind sweeps; innocent
As the Christ child – made flesh in paint
On pious old pictures – frail and small.

And be tough as the big wolves that bleed
From many wounds, yet live indeed.

1936

SONG OF DEATH
At the Funeral of Dezső Kosztolányi

A dank autumnal mist drips on the grave.
It is still day, and yet it seems like night.
The torches wreathe a web of heavy smoke
Sheer silver against the sky, it is so dark.

And way up there a startled songbird cries!
The soul is faltering – it's gripped with fear –
As fluttery as that light-winged cloud: the one
Whose chill the radiant stars breathe heat upon.

And silent in its pit the body rests.
It lives out the quiet dignity of clods.
It rots, to be drunk down by a parched root
And reborn as the green blaze underfoot –

So Law decrees! It is terrible, so terrible
That what was one world spins off into two.
Or is it wisdom? The body alone can know.
Defend, oh Lord, the pathways of the soul.

November 1936

HISPANIA, HISPANIA

I see, opening my window, the Paris rooftops glistening:
This downpour has kept going for two days.
A cloud has settled on my table; light
Runs moistly down my face.

Though above houses here, I am somehow in the depths.
Rain-sodden soot is weeping for me, confused
By a sense of shame at this twilight hour, bespattered
With heavy mud and news.

Oh soughing black-winged war,
Fear flying here from across the frontier!
They sow no corn here, neither do they reap,
Grapes rot awaiting the harvester.

The fledglings are all mute, there is no sun to blaze
And mothers are no longer bearing sons;
Only your foaming rivers, oh Hispania –
Swollen with blood they run.

But new armies will come, if need be out of nowhere;
Like furious whirlwinds they will sweep
Across the land from wounded fields and mines –
Arising from the deep.

Freedom, your fate is cried out by whole nations!
Today I also heard a sung refrain:
The Paris poor were singing of your struggle
In heavy words, their faces splashed with rain.

6 August 1937

Forest in October

There on the bush wet chaos breeds:
Still golden yesterday, dead leaves
Under the trees have turned to waste –
Brown mud that covers worms, snails, seeds
And a beetle's shattered carapace.

In vain you look around you – here
Terror has flooded everything:
A nervous squirrel squeals with fear,
Dropping his morsel through the air –
One bound, and he springs from limb to limb;

Learn to defend yourself, like him:
Nor will this wintry order care
For you, neither do archangels –
Like mother-of-pearl the light trembles,
And one by one your brethren die.

1937

29

LULLABY

People are murdered all the time,
   Somewhere – be it in the laps
Of dozy valleys, or on watchful peaks
   That peer; so what a cold comfort
To say 'Ah, but it's so far off!'
   Shanghai or Guernica –
Either is just as close to my heart
   As your small frightened hand,
Or the planet Jupiter, high above us.
   No don't look up at the sky,
Don't even look at the earth, just sleep.
   For death is racing through
The sparkling dust of the Milky Way
   And pouring molten silver
On headlong shadows tumbling down.

1937

IN THE MARGINS OF THE PROPHET HABAKKUK

Whole cities
Were ablaze,
Villages
Crashed in smoke.
Be with me,
Stern prophet
Habakkuk!

The cinders
Have now cooled,
Black as coal,
But there's fire
In me still:
It will bite
And burn bright.

Gall to me
Is my food
And drink. From
Head to foot,
Black rage, coat
Me with soot.

1937

PEACE, HORROR

When I stepped out through the gate, it was just ten o'clock,
A baker sped by on gleaming wheels, a song on his lips,
A plane droning high overhead and the sun up, it was ten,
And my dead sister came into my mind and with that they were all
Flying above me – those whom I love and who are not alive –
Darkly across the sky, a host of the silent dead . . .
Then, a jolt, and a shadow crumpled against the wall.
Silence. The morning came to a halt on the stroke of ten:
Hovering over the street, peace – and a certain horror.

1938

First Eclogue

Quippe ubi fas versum atque nefas: tot bella per orbem,
Tam multae scelerum facies . . .

Virgil

SHEPHERD
It's long since we last met here. Did the song of the thrushes call you?

POET
I'm listening to the woods: there is such a din now spring's here!

SHEPHERD
This isn't spring. The sky wants to fool us. Just look at this puddle:
Now it is smiling meekly, but at night when the frost congeals it
It'll bear its teeth! This is April: a fool's month to believe in.
Those little tulips there have been nipped in the bud by frost.
Why sad? Won't you sit down here on this stone beside me?

POET
It's not that I'm sad: I've grown so used to this terrible world
That sometimes I am not hurt by it – merely disgusted.

SHEPHERD

What I heard is now certain. On the ridges of the wild Pyrenees
Red-hot cannon wrangle amid corpses stiff with blood,
And bears join with the soldiers as they flee.
In flocks, with knotted bundles, flee old folk, women and children,
Throwing themselves to the ground as death starts circling above,
And there are so many lying dead, they are left there, no-one
     removes them.
I think you knew Federico. Did he escape, ah tell me!

POET

He did not flee. They killed him. Two years ago in Granada.

SHEPHERD

García Lorca is dead! And you are the first to tell me!
The news of war travels so fast, yet the poet
Can just disappear like that. Did Europe not mourn his death?

POET

It was not even noticed. At best, the wind in the pyre's ashes,
Groping, will find among them some broken line to remember.
This much is left, no more, to the curious who come after us.

SHEPHERD

He did not flee. He died. But then where can a poet escape?
Nor did our beloved Attila flee; he just said *No*
To the present state. And yet, who mourns him now he has fallen?
How do you live? Can your words still find an echo in these times?

POET
While cannon boom? Among smouldering ruins, deserted villages?
Still, I keep on writing and live in this frenzied world
As that oak over there: it knows it will be cut down and already
Is marked with a white cross, showing that there, tomorrow,
The woodcutter begins. Yet, as it waits, it puts forth a new leaf.
You are fortunate here: it's so still – few wolves come this way,
And as it is months since your master was here, you can often
Forget that the flock you tend belongs to somebody else.
God bless you. Time I get home, old night will have fallen upon me.
The butterfly dusk is fluttering, its wings shedding silver sift.

1938

In a Restless Hour

Windswept heights in the sunshine were my dwelling.
Oh homeland, now in a valley you have imprisoned
    The broken son you clothe in shadow,
        No heavenly play of sunlight here to soothe me.

Crags above me, glorious sky in the distance,
I must live in the depths with speechless boulders.
    Must I be dumb too? What would move me
        Now to poetry? Death? Who is it asks me,

Who calls me to a reckoning for my life
Or for this poem here, which remains a fragment?
    Know this: nobody will mourn you
        Or bury you, nor will the valley cradle

Or the wind scatter you. Yet the high cliff-side –
If not today, then tomorrow – will echo, singing,
    What I've to speak, which sons and daughters
        Will understand, the more as they grow in stature.

10 January 1939

WRITTEN IN A COPY OF *STEEP PATH*

I am a poet and unnecessary,
Even when, wordless, I go murmuring
Ti-tum ti-tum. Who cares? Instead of me,
The nosy little devils sing.

And oh, believe me, do! Not without reason,
Prudent suspicion fans my face like breath:
I am a poet, good for the stake alone,
As witness to the truth,

Who knows that snow is white, that blood is red
And that the poppy's flower is red as well,
With its fine, fuzzy stem green as the field,

Who knows that, in the end, he will be killed
Because he would not kill.

1 June 1939

SIMPLE SONG OF MY WIFE

As she comes in, cackles burst from the door,
The potted plants all stamp, shaking the floor,
A blond streak, small and drowsy, in her hair
Cheeps like a frightened sparrow in the straw.

Clumsily whirling towards her through the air,
The ageing light-flex too lets out a squawk:
Everything spins – to jot it down, no chance.

She has come back. She has been gone all day.
She bears an enormous poppy in her hands
To drive death, my adversary, away.

5 January 1940

FOAMING SKY

The moon bobs on the sky's foam.
I wonder at being alive tonight.
Assiduous death keeps searching our dark time
And those he finds are all unearthly white.

Sometimes the year looks back, lets out a scream,
Looks back, then passes out appalled.
Again what a grim autumn's crouched behind me
And what a winter, numbed by pain and dulled!

The forest bled and, in the cycle
Of time, each hour would shed its blood.
The wind scrawled numbers, vast and dark,
On snow-drifts in the wood.

I have come to see both that and this.
I feel how heavily air weighs on the earth.
A warm silence, alive with rustling noises,
Envelops me – as before birth.

I stop under a tree whose leaves
Seethe with anger. Its branches creak.
One reaches down – to grasp my throat?
I am no coward, nor am I weak,

But tired. I hold my tongue. The branch
Gropes through my hair in silence, fearfully.
I know we ought to forget, but I
Never forget a single memory.

The moon founders in foam. Across the sky
A dark-green track of poison has been driven.
I stand and roll myself a cigarette,
Slowly, carefully. I am living.

8 June 1940

In My Memories

Still walking in my memories, the flowers . . .
I stand there, spattered by the blustering showers.
Two women pass, who smile with glistening teeth;
     Then two pigeons – their round
Puffed-up, pompous bellies sweep the ground.

A year ago. The road toward Senlis.
In an odd way – the twilight mild and rainy –
I felt just for a moment happy again.
     Green walls confined my road,
The ferny woods swayed silently and bowed,

And down from Ermenonville, like a witless girl
In a white skirt, a young birch-grove whirled
Around the bend to greet us – where he stood,
     That soldier, as if posed,
On the mud-shimmers. Between his teeth, a rose.

As if some brilliance flashed across the sky . . .
Gyula sat facing me with gentle Zsuzsa,
Fanni beside me – the landscape passed us by
     In her blue eyes and the joyous
Mane of the motor-car flapped over us –

Then Paris awaiting, sweet at the day's end.
Since then, quick death has roared around that bend
And culled his bunch of many-coloured flowers.
     About the still-warm dead
The birch-grove loiters, blushing and blood-red,

And the soldier, trench-dweller, hero set apart,
Lies on his back, and a rose stems from his heart.
His country is on fire. Among the flames
   Sway brooding cemeteries . . .
Walls running with sweat, contorted trees.

Above them, through thick soot, the whole sky burns,
Yet all the stars at evening still return
And dawns, whose tears are dew, keep racing on
   Toward the silent day.
If I asked the landscape something, would it say?

Still walking in my memories, the flowers . . .
I stand there, spattered by the blustering showers.
Women with children flocking down the road,
   Smoke turning day to night –
A cloud ripple. It's clearing. Silver, light.

1940

Calendar

January

The sun is late in rising, the sky's still
Brimful with a dense darkness.
Black so floods it that, almost,
It overflows.
Ice splinters beneath the steps
Of dawn, who through the grey cold goes.

February

Snow flutters down once more, settles upon the ground,
Then finally melts; it trickles,
Carving its way on.
Now the sun flashes. The sky flashes too.
The sun flashes, blinks in the sky.
And hark! to this, in a white voice,
The flock bleats in reply,
And chirruping a sparrow shakes its feathers toward the blue.

March

Look! on the puddle are goose-pimples.
March, making a big noise,
Walks under the trees with sharp winds
Like wild and merry boys.
Weaving spiders are not yet out
Nor buds that feel the cold,
But yellow chicks already frisk about
Like balls of gold.

April

A breeze that has stepped on a glass splinter cries
And hops on one leg out of it.
Oh April, April, not yet
Does the sun shine, do the small buds –
Their noses always wet –
Unfold beneath the whistling-warbling skies.

May

A petal on a tree shivers and falls.
The coming-on of dusk brings whitish smells.
Down from the mountain cool night flows,
Trees walking through it in their leafy rows.
Now from the cold the slight warmth flees
And hides; the candles glow on chestnut trees.

June

Just look around and see a miracle.
Its brow quite smooth, the sky is bright. It's noon.
There's a gold crest on the stream now and all
The acacias by the roadside are in bloom.
With diamond body a big, devil-may-care
Braggart of a dragonfly is writing
Signals that flash on the bright summer air.

July

Fury, up there, cramps the cloud's belly –
The cloud pulls a face.
Showers of rain run about barefoot,
Wet hair all over the place.
They get tired, creep into the ground, and then
It is evening time.
And the heat, its body bathed, hangs over
The trees, whose faces shine.

August

The meadow's looking drenched
In the loud sun. Now you perceive
The yellow of golden apples
Gorgeous among the leaves.
In proud trees the red squirrel squeaks,
The chestnut prickles thick with spikes.

September

The Septembers I have known, mature in reason!
Under the trees lie the brown jewels that glisten:
So many chestnuts. Evoking Africa,
Her scorching plains – before the cooling rains.
Dusk making a bed on the grey clouds,
A drowsy light drizzles on tired trees.
Sweet autumn comes, her bound hair falling free.

October

Cool, golden, a wind flutters;
Folk sit down – they're wayfarers.
A mouse in the pantry gnaws;
Gold too, a high branch glisters.
All things here are yellow-gold;
Maize with yellow flags unfurled
(Though they are bedraggled, wet)
Waves them, daren't discard them yet.

November

The frost has come, it screams on the house wall.
The teeth of the dead click. The sound is clear.
And the short, greyish locks of the wild myrtle
Are rustling in the dry brown tree up there.
A portent falls on me – from a screech owl.
Am I afraid? Perhaps I am not, now.

December

At midday this silver moon,
At full, is the sun: a mere hint in the sky.
Fog drifts, a sluggish bird.
By night, there is snow falling and
An angel soughs through the dark, he is drawing nigh.
Now, over deep snow, death
Approaches, and is unheard.

14 January 1939 – 28 February 1941

Your Right Hand under My Neck

I lay in bed last night, your right hand under my neck.
I asked you not to remove it – my day must still have been aching.
I listened at your wrist to the sound of the blood pulsating.

It was near midnight, and sleep had already flooded over me.
It broke on me suddenly – as long ago in the sleepy
Years of my downy childhood – and it rocked me just as gently.

It was not – so you tell me now – even three o'clock yet when
I started up in terror, and sat there – in my sleep
Mumbling, then declaiming, then screaming unintelligibly,

And I flung my arms out wide, as a bird ruffled with fear
Will beat its wings when a shadow sweeps the garden
    unpredictably.
Where was I heading? Which way? What form of death was it
    scared me?

You were there comforting me, and I let you, sitting asleep,
And lay back in silence, though still with the road of terrors ahead.
And went on dreaming. Perhaps of some other death instead.

6 April 1941

47

Second Eclogue

PILOT
We went far last night. In rage, I laughed, I was so mad.
Their fighters were all droning like a bee-swarm overhead.
Their defence was strong and, friend, oh how they fired and fired –
Till over the horizon our relief squadron appeared.
I just missed being shot down and scraped together below,
But see! I am back and, tomorrow, this craven Europe shall know
Fear in its air-raid shelters, as they tremble hidden away . . .
But enough of that, let's leave it. Have you written since yesterday?

POET
I have. The poet writes, as dogs howl or cats mew
Or small fish coyly spawn. What else am I to do?
I write about everything – write even for you, up there,
So that flying you may know of my life and of how I fare
When between the rows of houses, blown up and tumbling down,
The bloodshot light of the moon reels drunkenly around,
When the city squares bulge, all of them terror-stricken,
Breathing stops, and even the sky will seem to sicken,
And the planes keep coming on, then disappear, and then
Swoop, like jabbering madness, down from the sky again.
I write; what else can I do? If you knew how dangerous
A poem can be, how frail, how capricious a single verse . . .
For that involves courage too – you see? Poets must write,
Cats mew, dogs howl, small fish . . . and so on; but you who fight,
What do you know? Nothing. You listen, but all you hear
Is the plane you have just left, as it drones on in your ear.
No use denying it, friend. It's become a part of you.
What do you think about as you fly above in the blue?

48

PILOT

Laugh at me, but I'm scared. And I long to lie in repose
Beside my love on a bed, and for these eyes to close.
Or else, under my breath, I would softly hum her a tune
In the wild and steamy chaos of the flying-men's canteen.
Up there I want to come down, down here to be back in space:
In this world moulded for me, for me there is no place.
And I know full well, I have grown too fond of my aeroplane –
True, but if hit, the rhythm we suffer at is the same . . .
But you know and will write about it! It won't be a secret that I,
Who now just destroy, homeless between the earth and the sky,
Lived as a man lives. Alas, who'd understand or believe it?
Will you write of me?

POET

        If I live, if there's anyone left to read it.

27 April 1941

Third Eclogue

My pastoral Muse, be with me here, although I'm sitting
In a sleepy café. Out there, light flashes by and, in the fields,
Moles burrow silently, their molehills hump the land,
And tanned fishermen, handsome in body, their teeth white,
Are asleep, their dawn's work done, on their boats' slippery boards.

My pastoral Muse, be with me in this city grove here too.
Seven salesmen blab on noisily – but *they* shouldn't scare you off
For believe me, these forlorn lads are even now burdened with troubles . . .
And look at those on my right, they are jurists all and although
Not one can play on the flute, how they puff at their big cigars!

Be with me now! I was teaching and rushed in here between lessons
To brood on the wonder of love on the wings of all this smoke.
I thought that this would revive me, as the squeaky pipe of a bird
Might revive a withered tree. It transported me to what once
Were the heights of my youth and the wilds of adolescent desire.

Pastoral Muse, be my helper! For the fanfares of dawn
Proclaim her, blare of her form in a full, in a misty tone:
How her body glows, in her eyes the hint of a smile sparkles,
How a sigh comes to her lips with the nimble steps of a dance,
How she moves, how she embraces, how she looks up at the moon!

Pastoral Muse, help me! At last, let me sing of love.
Sorrow claws at me, new pains pursue me through this world –
New ones again and again. Soon I shall perish here.
Trees grow crooked, the mouths of salt-mines are caving in,
Bricks cry out in the wall: all this I dream of nightly.

Pastoral Muse, oh assist me! How poets die in this age . . .
The sky falls in on us, no tumuli mark our ashes,
No Greek urns, graceful in form, preserve them. Only poems –
A couple if any – survive us . . . Can I still write of love?
I see how her body shines. Oh help me, pastoral Muse!

12 June 1941

SKIN AND BONE AND PAIN
On the death of Mihály Babits

I

At last, after so much suffering, behold
This brownish body, cooled now and at rest:
Just skin and bone, and pain.
Like a tree-trunk, in its fall torn apart
And showing its growth-rings,
It too confesses its tormented years.
No more than skin and bone.

And now the nation's body
Is likewise skin and bone and pain. He'd pray
To you, St Blaise, so fold him in your arms.
O requiem aeternam dona ei . . . Domine!

II

Gather around him, words. His own words first:
Come like the foam cresting the waves of pain.
Come all of you, words bobbing in the dark
Of the mind dulled with grief,
And stay with me.
Mourn him, you crumbling *clods*
And shower his grave.
Oh come, tenuous *veil*,
And cover him.
And him, abandoned long by his own voice,
Mourn too, oh tolling *bell*.
You too, aspiring *soul*, you, perfect *pearl*,

Mourn him; and mourn again,
Oh *star*, you sparkling word, and you,
Who peer so slowly from the night, oh *moon*:
All words of his, all mourn!

III

We had long known there was no hope: with the cancer
Gnawing at you, in your eyes shone the light
Of a far world, spun of eternal things,
Where you are timeless as the stars at night.

We knew that you would die, and yet we stayed
Here on the earth, the orphans of your work.
Its magnitude exemplary. Its height,
Its dizzying force. It drives the pounding heart.

IV

Who will now watch over our pen hands?
You'd examine, tired and ill, our every line . . .
Who for us now will be the living Measure?
Look, how the pain's already broken up
This verse of mine.

How would you judge it? Even the coming poet,
Advancing timidly, is at your pleasure,
Your Work the measure.

And he won't understand that it's as orphans
We nod: Yes, he has gone . . . It is too hard.
He did not know you, sit beside your bed,
Or share your board.

He can't know what it is that painfully
Touches us all, will not ask or be asked . . .
It won't be as for years with us, when we
Have given the password: 'Who's been out to him?
What news of Mihály Babits? How is he?'

V

No longer can his dead hand hold the pen.
No more will nights be seen with his closed eyes.
Eternal light, a heavenly flame unfurling
Across the earth's dark smoke toward him flies.

August – September 1941

AUTUMN BEGINS RESTLESSLY

Restless the sun erupts, it's lapped today
By iron-grey, fire-fringed flags.
Its vapours stream down, and the floating light
Bites into louring fogs.

The clouds are ruffled. The smooth pane of the sky
Ripples in the wind, as the blue flies away.
The low flight of a swallow preparing to leave
Describes a screaming 'e' or 'a'.

Autumn begins restlessly: the leaves,
Dying in rust, are flailing up and down
And the sky's breath is cool.
The air gives off no warmth – nothing but smoke.
The sun no more than sighs today, and feebly.

A lizard scuttles on the great graveyard wall.
Autumn's ravening wasps,
Gorging on flesh, are buzzing rabidly.

Men on the banked earth
Of trenches sit and stare
At the deep fires of death.
The smell of heavy leaf-mould floats on the air.

Flame flies above the road –
Half-light, half-blood, it flares on the coming dark.
Brown leaves burning in the wind
Flutter, spark.

And clustered grapes weigh on the vine, the vine-shoots wilt.
Drily the stems of yellow flowers
Crackle, and seeds fall to the ground.

The meadow is swimming in the evening mist.
At length, the wild clattering sound
Of distant carts shakes from the trees
The few leaves that persist.

The landscape falls asleep.
Death, lovely in his white glide,
Settles on the countryside.
The sky cradles the garden.
Look: in your hair's an autumn leaf that's golden.
Above you, branches weep.

Ah but your flame must rise above death and autumn
And raise me, love, along with you.
Let the wise thing be to love me today –
Be wise and kiss me, hungry for dreams too.

Joyfully love me, do not leave me, fall
With me into the dark sky sleep creates.
Let's sleep. Out there, the thrush is well asleep.
The walnut, falling on fallen leaves piled deep,
Makes no harsh sound. Reason disintegrates.

10 October 1941

SIMILES

What you are like when you bend over me
Is a whispering bough.
And you are like a poppy too,
Your flavour is a mystery.

And then as time's unending wave upon wave
You are enthralling;
Also as calming as
A stone set on a grave.

You are like a friend I grew up with. Yet still
Even today I do not
Utterly know your hair,
Its fragrant weight and smell.

Sometimes, drifting tenuous as smoke,
You're blue, and I fear you'll leave me.
Sometimes you scare me when you turn
The colour of a lightning-stroke

And sombre gold – like sunlight flaring through
A sky the storm makes war in.
Whenever you are angry
You are the vowel *u* –

Dark, and far-resonant, and deep-voiced;
And at such times,
I draw bright loops fashioned of smiles around you
Till you are noosed.

16 November 1941

57

SPRING FLIES
Prelude to the Eclogues

Ice glides down the river: the bank darkens, blotched with thaw.
The snow is melting. Now, the infant sunbeams paddle
In the small puddles forming in tracks of roebuck and hare.
Spring flies, her hair streaming, over recumbent hills;
Deep down in the mine-shafts and the moles' burrows
She runs along roots of trees and under the buds' soft armpits,
Rests on the stalks of trembling leaves, then rushes on.
And over the meadows, on the hill's ripple, over rippling lakes, the sky
        With a blue flame is flickering by.

Spring flies with her hair streaming, but the angel of past freedom
No longer flies beside her, he is sleeping deep down, frozen
In yellow mud: unconscious, he lies among stunned roots.
He sees no light down there, not even the troops of tiny
Green leaves from shrubs unfurling. It's hopeless, he will not waken.
He's a captive. And splash in his dream goes the harsh sorrow of prisoners,
Blackly it swirls – his heart burdened by frosty night and earth.
He dreams and, down there, not even a sigh, not yet, makes his chest rise
        To crack the ice in which he lies.

Cry out, dumb roots! Oh leaves, cry out in a shrill voice!
Dog, bay, as you froth at the mouth! Fish, beat the foam!
Horse, shake your mane! Bull, roar! Riverbed, weep!
        Awake at last, oh sleeping one!

11 April 1942

NIGHT

The heart is asleep and, in the heart, anxiety.
The fly is asleep near the cobweb on the wall.
The house is quiet: not a scratch from a wakeful mouse.
The garden sleeps, the branch, the woodpecker in the trunk,
The beetle sleeps in the rose, the bee in the hive
And summer in the wheat-grains that are scattering.
Flame sleeps in the moon too, cold medal on the sky.
Autumn is up and, to steal, goes stealthily by.

1 June 1942

Fourth Eclogue

POET
When I was still unborn, if you'd only asked . . .
Oh I knew then, I knew!
I howled: 'I don't want the world, it is so harsh!
Darkness clubs me, then light cuts me through.'
And I survived. My skull soon knit, hardening with the years.
And my lungs were only strengthened by all those bawling tears.

VOICE
You were washed ashore, threshing about
On blood-red waves of measles and scarlet fever.
A lake once made to gulp you down, but spat you out.
What do you think? Why did time take you into his arms?
And your lungs with their wing-span, your heart, your liver –
This warm, moist, mysterious machine
Serves you . . . But why? And cancer may not yet begin
To bloom, terrible flower, beneath your healthy skin.

POET
I was born. I protested. And yet, here I am.
I grew up. You ask me why? I cannot say.
I've always wanted to be free, and guards
Have always marched beside me on my way.

VOICE
You have been to peaks blown radiant by the wind,
And you saw at dusk a doe in piety
Kneel between shrubs that clung to the mountain-side.
You saw a drop of amber on the sunlit trunk of a tree,
And once a great stag-beetle settled upon your hand.
You saw a naked girl in the stream, stepping ashore . . .

POET
In bondage I can see such things no more.
I wish I had been a hill, a bird, a flower,
A comforting butterfly-thought,
A God-mimicking moment. Help me, freedom,
At last to find a place to make my home in.

That peak again, the woods, the shrubs, the woman,
The wings of spirit burning in the wind!
And into a new world to be re-born,
When the sun, blinding, with its light diffused
Through golden vapours, shall rise to a new dawn.

It is quiet, it is still quiet, but the storm's breath
Can be felt, and the ripe fruit's swaying on the boughs.
The butterfly is borne on a light breeze.
It flies. Now death is blowing through the trees.

And now I know: I too ripen for death.
The waves of time that raised me pitch me down.
I was once a prisoner, and my loneliness
Is waxing slowly like the crescent moon.

I shall be free: earth grants me absolution,
And blazing over the earth my shattered world
Floats slowly. The tables of stone have been cracked.
Rise up on your heavy wings, oh imagination!

VOICE
The fruit is swaying. Once ripe, it will fall.
The deep earth, stored with memories, will lull you where you lie.
But let the smoke of your wrath fly up to heaven when all
Is ruined here – to write across the sky.

15 March 1943

The Terrible Angel

The terrible angel that I have within,
Today unseen and silent, does not scream.
There is a sound though – I prick up my ears –
Slight as a grasshopper's. So I turn
And look: who was it? Don't know. Well, it's him.
He's being cautious once more. Getting ready.
Protect me, if you love me: brave and steady.
He hides when you are with me. When you leave,
He takes new heart. He rises without reason
From the soul's depth and hurls out accusations.
Insanity. He works in me like poison
And seldom sleeps. He lives
Within me and without. When moonbeams lave
The dark with white, he'll run,
His sandals shushing through the grassy fields,
To scrabble wildly in my mother's grave
And wake her. 'Was it worth it?' he will say,
Disturbing her, inciting her with whispers:
'You died of giving birth to him!' He'll glance
From time to time at me and, in advance,
Tear off the waiting pages in the calendar.
The how and when and where
Are henceforth in his hands. It was his word
Fell in my heart last night: as when a stone
Plops into water, just like that I heard
It floating, swirling, making rings. Alone,
You sleeping and me watching, I'd undressed
And so was naked when
By night he came and in a soft voice pressed

His arguments upon me once again.
The weirdest odour floated on the air,
A cold breath nipped my ear and 'Just keep on
Stripping,' he urged. 'Shed your protective layer.
For exposed nerve is what you are, raw flesh.
Flay yourself; for the fool
Who boasts of his own skin boasts of his gaol.
Your skin is but a vesture. This knife' – he pointed –
'Takes a split second, it's painless, a mere slash.'

And on the board the knife awoke and glinted.

4 August 1943

Paris

Where the pavement of the Boulevard St Michel
Turns into Rue Cujas, there's a slight camber.
Oh time of youth, so wild and beautiful,
I've not forsaken you: my heart remembers
Like a mine-shaft your voice's resonance.
Our baker had his shop on Rue Monsieur le Prince.

And to the left, where the park trees show tall,
One tree was yellowing against the sky,
As if already it had glimpsed the fall.
Freedom, oh cherished nymph with the long thigh,
Are you still hiding in the twilight gold
Among the veiling trees, just as you were of old?

Summer was like an army marching in
To drumbeats, sweating, raising dust on the road.
A cool mist followed in its tracks, and then
To either side of it a fragrance flowed.
Noon was still summertime; come afternoon,
Sweet autumn visited behind a front of rain.

In those days I enjoyed a life unbound
As a child does, yet I was one who'd know,
Like an old pedant, that the earth was round.
I was green still but with a beard like snow.
I wandered freely. Whom would it concern?
Then, going underground, I felt the deep fires burn.

Where are you now, oh stations of time past:
CHATELET – CITE – ST MICH' and ODEON?
Then DENFERT-ROCHEREAU – like a name cursed.
The map that flowered on the stained wall is gone.
I shout: Where are you? And I strain to hear,
As if the sweat and ozone were roaring in my ear.

And then the nights! Those wanderings by night
From the outskirts toward the Quartier!
Will dawn ever again with its strange light
Pierce through the dull sky as a soft grey,
As when, from poetising, drunk in the head,
I undressed half-asleep and fell into my bed?

If only I had the strength just to return
And skip the headlong current of my fate!
The cat from the cheap, smelly restaurant
Downstairs would go up on the roof to mate.
The noise it made! Will I, just once again,
Hear that? For then I learned in what a din
Noah, so long ago, floated beneath the moon.

14 August 1943

Just as Unnoticed

Just as unnoticed as the way we lapse into sleep
Is the lapse from youth to manhood, as unapparent.
You've acquired a past, you sit down to some hard drinking,
And more and more of your friends have become parents.

When the father calls on you now, he brings his little son,
And gradually it's the boy who, more than his father,
Understands you and all the adventures of your fevered heart,
As you mock time's pendulum on the floor together.

Still, sometimes you earn a living as grown-ups do:
You sell a poem, you're commissioned to translate,
You can only make ends meet with the help of 'extras',
You try to unravel a contract, you protest, you calculate.

To flirt with Lady Fortune would make no difference:
Only those who arrive at the right time she favours.
You care less for honey and walnuts, which tempt the brooding youth,
Than for purple morello cherries and poppy-seed – bitterish flavours.

And no matter how much the heated brain may dance and delude,
You know that even in summer a leaf can fall from the bough
And that once you are dead all things are weighed in the balance.
You can't be a champion sportsman or a roving mariner now,

But that the pen is tool and weapon, that to play an honest lute
Worthily you may risk your neck – these you have learned;
And that even in this way, you can get to any land where
Purpose is naked and the fires of adventure burn.

And as you press down on your pen, you think of children
And now in your heavy heart you can't feel proud,
For you work for them like men in factories that creak
With silent dust, and men in workshops whose backs are bowed.

15 November 1943

FIFTH ECLOGUE

In Memory of György Bálint
(Fragment)

My dear friend, how the cold of this poem made me shiver,
How afraid I was of words. Today, too, I have fled it.
Have scribbled half-lines.
                     I tried to write about something –
About anything else, but in vain. This furtive night of terror
Admonishes: 'Speak of him.'
                    And I start up, but the voice
Is silent again – like the dead, out there on Ukrainian fields.
You're missing.
          And autumn's brought no news of you.
                             Again
Wild prophecy of winter soughs through the forest, clouds
Fly heavy across the sky, till snow-laden they stop.
Alive still? Who knows?
           Now *I* don't, and I don't flare with rage
When people shake their heads or in pain hide their faces.
And they know nothing.
            But are you alive? Or just wounded?
Are you walking through fallen leaves and the odour of forest mud
Or are you yourself but a fragrance?
                Snow flutters over the fields.
'Missing' – the news thuds home.
             And my heart thumps once, then freezes.
Between two of my ribs, at such times, there's a pain that tenses and throbs,
Words you said long ago now live in my mind as clearly
And I feel your bodily presence, right here, as vividly
As if you were dead . . .
          And today, I still can't write of you.

21 November 1943

69

I Cannot Tell

I cannot tell what this land means for others. For me,
This little country ringed by fire's the mother-land –
The far-off world of childhood rocking in the distance.
I have grown from it like a frail branch from a tree
And my hope is that my body will sink into earth here.
I'm at home here. And whenever a bush kneels at my feet,
I'll know its name for sure, know the name of the flower.
I know where all the people who walk down the road are going,
And in the summer sunset I know what that sore means,
That reddens as it trickles down the walls of every house.
For a man flying over it this land is just a map.
He wouldn't know, for instance, where Vörösmarty lived.
What would the map hide for him? A factory, the tough barracks.
For me there are oxen, grasshoppers, a steeple, and gentle farms.
Through binoculars he would see a factory or the fields.
I see the worker trembling, fearful for his job,
Orchards abrim with birdsong, vineyards, a forest, graves,
An old woman among the graves, who's softly weeping.
And what from above is a railway or plant marked for destruction
Is merely a signal-box, the keeper out in front of it
With a red signal-flag, many children around him
And a sheepdog that rolls on the ground in the factory yard.
And there's the park and, in it, the footprints of old flames –
I taste their kisses still, now honey, now blackberries.
And once on my way to school I walked on the pavement's edge
And trod – to forestall being tested – on one propitious stone:
Here is that stone. But up there, you're too high to make it out –
There's no device to reveal such things as that with precision.

70

True, we are all guilty, like the people of other nations,
And we know where our fault lies – when, how and where we did wrong.
But workers live here too, and poets who labour in innocence,
And tiny babies in whom reason is young, is growing –
It shines in them, they protect it – as they hide in the dark shelters –
For the day when the finger of peace marks out our land for deliverance
And with fresh words they will answer our talk, which is muffled, hushed.

Night cloud, in your vigil, spread your great wings over us.

17 January 1944

Oh Ancient Prisons

Oh peace of ancient prisons, beautiful
    Outmoded suffering, the heroic stance
Sublimely struck, the poet's death, and all
    Such measured speech as finds an audience –
How far away they are. Whoever dares
    Even move, steps in the void. A foggy blur.
Reality, like damaged earthenware,
    Bulges and waits for the one thing to occur:
To be reduced to shards and rottenness.
    How will it be for him who for the time
    He lives – allowed to – speaks in measured rhyme
And teaches judgement of whatever *is?*

    And would teach still. But all things fall apart.
    He sits and stares: is utterly inert.

27 March 1944

Neither Memory, nor Magic

There was all that anger hidden here in my heart before,
As the seeds dark as Africans hide in an apple-core,
And I knew there was an angel walking, sword in hand, behind me –
There in my time of trouble to guard me and defend me.
But if, some wild dawn hour, you should awake to find
Your world in ruins and, your few things left behind,
Should set forth almost naked, a ghost in the dawn glow –
Then in your fine and lightly-pacing heart there'll start to grow
A mature humility, reflective, sparing of speech;
When you do speak rebellion, it'll be disinterested
And in hope of a free future shining from far ahead.

I never did have anything and never shall do now.
Consider for a moment how wealthy my life is, how
Little I seek revenge, there being no anger in my heart;
The world will be rebuilt and where the new walls start
My song, which is now banned, will be heard again, my voice.
I live through in myself all that will come to pass.
I shall look back no more, for I know: nothing can save me,
Neither memory, nor magic – the sky lours above me.
Friend, if you see me, shrug, then turn your back on me.
Where the angel with his sword was standing once
There may be nobody.

30 April 1944

FRAGMENT

I lived on this earth in an age
When man fell so low he killed with pleasure
And willingly, not merely under orders.
His life entangled, trapped, in wild obsession,
He trusted false gods, raving in delusion.

I lived on this earth in an age
That esteemed informers, in an age whose heroes
Were the murderer, the bandit and the traitor.
And such as were silent – or just slow to applaud –
Were shunned as if plague-stricken, and abhorred.

I lived on this earth in an age
When any who spoke out would have to flee –
Forced to lie low and gnaw their fists in shame.
The folk went mad and, drunk on blood, filth, hate,
Could only grin at their own hideous fate.

I lived on this earth in an age
When a curse would be the mother of a child
And women were glad if their unborn miscarried.
The living – with poison seething on his plate –
Would envy the grave-dweller the worms eat.

....

I lived on this earth in an age
When poets too were silent: waiting in hope
For the great Prophet to rise and speak again –
Since no one could give voice to a fit curse
But Isaiah himself, scholar of terrible words.

19 May 1944

74

Seventh Eclogue

You see? As dark comes on, the barracks and the grim oak fence,
Girded with barbed-wire, dissolve: night soaks them up.
Slowly the eye relinquishes the bounds of our captivity
And the mind, only the mind, can tell how taut the wire is.
You see, dear? Even the fancy has no other way to freedom.
The broken body's released by the fair deliverer, sleep,
And the whole prison-camp, then, takes flight for home.
In rags, with their heads shaven, snoring, the prisoners fly
From the blind heights of Serbia to homelands now in hiding.
Homelands in hiding! Ah, does *our* home still exist?
It might have escaped the bombs? It still is – as when we left it?
Will that man who moans on my right, and this on my left, reach home?
Is there a land still, tell me, where this verse form has meaning?

Without putting in the accents, just groping line after line,
I write this poem here, in the dark, just as I live,
Half-blind, like a caterpillar inching my way across paper.
Torches, books – the guards have taken everything –
And no post comes, just fog, that settles over the barracks.

Among false rumours and worms, we live here with Frenchmen, Poles,
Loud Italians, heretic Serbs, nostalgic Jews, in the mountains.
This feverish body, dismembered but still living one life, waits
For good news, for women's sweet words, for a life both free and human,
And the end plunged into obscurity, and miracles.

A captive beast among worms, I lie on a plank. The fleas
Once more renew their assault, though the flies have gone to rest.
It's night, you see: captivity now is a day shorter.
And so is life. The camp is asleep. Over the land
The moon shines: in its light, the wires go taut again.
Through the window you can see how the shadows of armed guards
Go pacing along on the wall through the noises of the night.

The camp's asleep. You see, dear? Dreams fan their wings.
Somebody starts and groans, turns in his tight space and
Is already asleep again, his face aglow. I only
Sit up awake – on my lips, instead of your kisses, the taste
Of a half-smoked cigarette; and no sleep comes bringing rest,
For I can no longer die without you, nor can I live.

Lager Heideman, in the mountains above Žagubica
July 1944

LETTER TO MY WIFE

Deep down there, worlds dumb and silent lie:
The silence howling in my ears, I cry
But no one here can answer me in far
Serbia, stunned and crumpled into war.
And you are far off. Twined around my dreams
Is your voice, which by day my heart reclaims.
So I am silent. Cool to the touch and proud,
The many ferns around me hum aloud.

When I can see you once again – who were
Lovely as light, lovely as shadow, sure
And grave as a psalm is – I do not know.
Were I blind and dumb, I'd find you even so.
My mind projects you: in landscape you hide
But flash upon my eyes from deep inside.
You are but a dream again now, who were real;
My youthful self – I fall back down that well

And beg you 'Do you love me?' jealously,
And hope again that one day you will be
(When I have reached my prime of youth) my wife.
I fall back on the road of conscious life
Then, for I know you are. My wife and friend.
Three cruel frontiers, though, have intervened.
Slowly it's autumn. Will that too leave me here?
The memory of our kisses grows more clear;

I once believed in miracles – now though
I forget their dates . . . Above me bombers go . . .
I was just admiring your eyes' blue in the sky
But clouds came and a plane up there flew by
With bombs longing to fall. A prisoner,
I live despite them. All I have hopes for
I've thought out, yet I'll find my way to you,
For I have walked the soul's full length for you –

And the roads of all these lands. Through scarlet ash
I'll charm my way if need be, through the crash
Of worlds on fire – and yet I shall get back.
If need be, I'll be tough as a tree's bark,
And the calm that hardened men have, who each hour
Know danger, stress – a calm worth guns and power –
Soothes me and, like a cool wave of the sea,
Sobering, 'two-times-two' breaks over me.

Lager Heideman
August – September 1944

Root

Power flashes unseen through the root
That drinks rain, feeds on earth below;
And its dream is white as snow.

Its path thrust up from underground,
It is sly, this root, it creeps –
With its many arms like ropes.

Worms are sleeping on its arms,
To one leg a worm has stuck:
The world begins to teem with worms.

Not concerned with the world – just
With a branch hung thick with leaves –
Still, down there, the root survives.

This branch it adores and nurtures,
Sending up to it good flavours,
Sweet, heavenly flavours.

Now I am a root myself,
I am living among worms –
That is where I write these lines.

Once flower above, now root below:
Earth weighs upon me, dark and low.
This was ordained my destiny.
A saw is wailing over me.

Lager Heideman
8 August 1944

A la Recherche

You too, past gentle evenings, are being refined into memory!
Bright table, once adorned by poets and their young women,
Where in the mud of the past, now, do you slide away to?
Where is the night when friends, sparkling with wit and gusto,
Still drank their fine hock gaily from bright-eyed slender glasses?

Lines of poetry swam around in the lamplight, brilliant
Green adjectives swayed on the metre's foaming crest and
Those who are dead now were living, the prisoners still home, and all of
Those dear friends who are missing, the long-ago fallen, wrote poems.
Their hearts are under the soil of Flanders, Ukraine and Iberia.

There were men of a kind who gritted their teeth, ran into gunfire
And fought: only because they could do nothing against it.
And while the company – the filthy night their shelter –
Slept restlessly round them, they'd be thinking of rooms they'd lived in:
Islands and caves to them inside this hostile order.

There were places they travelled to in tight-sealed cattle-wagons.
They had to stand in minefields: they were unarmed and freezing.
There was a place they went to, guns in their hands and willing,
Without a word: they saw their own cause in that struggle.
And now the angel of freedom guards their deep dream nightly.

There were places . . . No matter. Where are the wise, wine-drinking parties?
Their call-up papers flew to them, fragmentary poems multiplied,
And wrinkles multiplied, too, around the lips and under
The eyes of young women with lovely smiles: sylph-like in bearing,
Those girls grew to be heavy in the silent years of wartime.

Where is the night, the bar, the table under the lime-trees?
And those still alive, where are they – those herded into the battle?
My hand still clasps their hands, my heart still hears their voices.
I recall their works, I perceive the stature of their torsos
Which appear to me, silent prisoner, on the wailing heights of Serbia.

Where is the night? That night will never more come back to us,
For whatever has passed on, death alters its perspectives.
They sit down at the table, they hide in the smiles of women,
And will sip wine from our glasses: they who now, unburied,
Sleep in far-away forests, sleep in distant pastures.

Lager Heideman
17 August 1944

Eighth Eclogue

POET

Hail! How well you endure this rugged mountain walk,
Fine old man. Is it that wings lift you or enemies hunt you?
Wings bear you, passion drives you, lightning flares in your eyes.
Hail, venerable elder! You are one, I now perceive,
Of the ireful prophets of old – but tell me, which of their number?

PROPHET

Which am I? I am Nahum the Elkoshite. It was I
Who thundered against the concupiscent city of Nineveh, I
Who declaimed the word of the Lord, his brimming vessel of anger.

POET

I know your ancient fury – your writings have been preserved.

PROPHET

They have. But more than of old, today, sin multiplies,
Yet even today there is no one who knows what the Lord's end is.
For the Lord said he would cause the abundant rivers to dry up,
Bashan to languish, and Carmel, and Lebanon's flower to wither,
The mountains would quake – all things would be consumed in fire.
And all this has befallen.

POET

To the slaughter nations scramble.
And the soul of man is stripped bare, even as Nineveh.
What use had admonitions? And the savage ravening locusts
In their green clouds, what effect? Of all beasts man is the basest.
Here, tiny babes are dashed against walls and, over there,
The church tower is a torch, the house an oven roasting
Its own people. Whole factories fly up in their smoke.
The street runs mad with people on fire, then swoons with a wail,
The vast bomb-bays disgorge, the great clamps loose their burdens
And the dead lie there, shrivelled, spattering city squares
Like a herd's dung on the pasture: everything, once again,
Has happened as you foretold. What brings you back here, tell me,
To earth from ancient cloud-swirl?

PROPHET

Wrath: that man as ever
Is an orphan again among the hosts of the seeming-human,
The heathen. And I wish again to see the strongholds of sin
Fall – wish to bear witness for the ages yet to come.

POET

You have already done so. The Lord spoke through you long ago:
Cried woe to the fortress filled with the spoils of war – with bastions
Built of corpses! But tell me, can it be so that fury
Has survived in you these millennia – with divine, unquenchable blaze?

PROPHET

There was a time when the Lord touched my unclean lips
As he did the sage Isaiah's. With his ember hovering over me
God probed my heart. The coal was a live coal and red-hot –
An angel held it with tongs and 'Look, here am I: let me
Also be called upon to preach thy word,' I cried after him.
And once a man has been sent by the Lord, he has no age,
He has no peace. That coal, angelic, burns on in his lips.
And what is a thousand years to the Lord? A mayfly time!

POET

How young you are, father! I envy you. What is my own brief time
To your awesome age? Even these few fleeting moments
Are wearing me down – like a round stone in a wild stream.

PROPHET

So you may think. But I know your new poems. Wrath nurtures you.
The poet's wrath, like the prophet's, it is food and drink
To the people. Whoever would may live on it until
The coming of the kingdom that young disciple promised,
The young rabbi whose life fulfilled our words and the law.
Come with me to preach that already the hour is at hand,
The kingdom about to be born. 'What,' I asked before,
'Is the Lord's end?' Lo, it is that kingdom. Come let us go:
Gather the people together. Bring your wife. Cut staffs.
Staffs for the wanderer are good companions. Look:
That one, let me have that one: I like the gnarled ones better.

Lager Heideman
23 August 1944

84

FORCED MARCH

A fool he is who, collapsed,   rises and walks again,
Ankles and knees moving   alone, like wandering pain,
Yet he, as if wings uplifted him,   sets out on his way,
And in vain the ditch calls him   back, who dare not stay.
And if asked why not, he might answer   – without leaving his path –
That his wife was awaiting him,   and a saner, more beautiful death.
Poor fool! He's out of his mind: now, for a long time,
Only scorched winds have whirled   over the houses at home,
The wall has been laid low,   the plum-tree is broken there,
The night of our native hearth   flutters, thick with fear.
Oh if only I could believe   that everything of worth
Were not just in my heart –   that I still had a home on earth;
If only I had! As before,   jam made fresh from the plum
Would cool on the old verandah,   in peace the bee would hum,
And an end-of-summer stillness   would bask in the drowsy garden,
Naked among the leaves   would sway the fruit-trees' burden,
And Fanni would be waiting,   blonde, by the russet hedgerow,
As the slow morning painted   slow shadow over shadow –
Could it perhaps still be?   The moon tonight's so round!
Don't leave me friend, shout at me: I'll get up off the ground!

15 September 1944

85

POSTCARDS

I

From Bulgaria, wild and swollen, the noise of cannon rolls;
It booms against the ridge, then hesitates, and falls.
Men, animals, carts, thoughts pile up as they fly;
The road rears back and whinnies, maned is the racing sky.
But you in this shifting chaos are what in me is constant:
In my soul's depth forever, you shine – you are as silent
And motionless as an angel who marvels at destruction,
Or a beetle burrowing in a hollow tree's corruption.

In the mountains
30 August 1944

II

No more than six or seven miles away
Haystacks and houses flare;
There, on the meadow's verges, peasants crouch,
Pipe-smoking, dumb with fear.
Here still, where the tiny shepherdess steps in,
Ripples on the lake spread;
A flock of ruffled sheep bend over it
And drink the clouds they tread.

Cservenka
6 October 1944

86

III

Blood-red, the spittle drools from the oxen's mouths,
The men stooping to urinate pass blood,
The squad stands bunched in groups whose reek disgusts.
And loathsome death blows overhead in gusts.

Mohács
24 October 1944

IV

I fell beside him. His body – which was taut
As a cord is, when it snaps – spun as I fell.
Shot in the neck. 'This is how you will end,'
I whispered to myself. 'Keep lying still.
Now, patience is flowering into death.'
'*Der springt noch auf*,' said someone over me.
Blood on my ears was drying, caked with earth.

Szentkirályszabadja
31 October 1944

NOTES

'Garden on Istenhegy'
Istenhegy is a hill on the Buda side of Budapest, where Fanni Radnóti's family owned a weekend cottage.

'Song of Death'
This poem was written after the funeral of Dezső Kosztolányi (1885–1936), a major Hungarian poet and writer. He belonged to the first generation associated with the periodical *Nyugat* (West), which played a pivotal role in the modernisation of Hungarian literature.

'Hispania, Hispania'
Written in Paris in the summer of 1937. Radnóti had just taken part in a Popular Front demonstration in solidarity with the Spanish Republic.

'Peace, Horror'
Written in 1938, this short poem reflects the shock felt in Hungary after the *Anschluss*, the annexation of Austria by the Third Reich.

'First Eclogue'
The first of a cycle of eight Eclogues composed between 1938 and 1944. The sixth eclogue is missing, though some critics have identified it as the poem entitled 'Fragment', p.74.

the wild Pyrenees: The Shepherd describes scenes from the final stage of the Spanish Civil War, when the Republican forces were driven north towards the French frontier.

I think you knew Federico: Federico García Lorca (1898–1936). See Introduction, pp.15–16.

our beloved Attila: Attila József (1905–37) was a left-wing poet, much admired by Radnóti. He was a persistent critic of 'the present state' – i.e. the Horthy regime. Mentally ill towards the end of his life, he committed suicide by throwing himself under a train.

'Written in a Copy of *Steep Path*'
Steep Path was a collection of Radnóti's poems, published in 1938.

'In My Memories'
Radnóti here recalls his last visit to France. Gyula (pronounced *Djoo*-lah) is Gyula Ortutay, a folklorist and friend of the poet's, and Zsuzsa (pronounced *Zhoo*-zha) was Ortutay's wife. Fanni (pronounced *Fun*-ni) was Radnóti's wife.

'Your Right Hand under My Neck'
This poem was written a few days after the Hungarian government allowed German troops to cross the country and invade Yugoslavia. On 3 April 1941, the then Prime Minister Count Pál Teleki, who had tried to preserve Hungary's neutrality, committed suicide in protest.

'Skin and Bone and Pain'
Mihály Babits (1886–1941), poet, writer, essayist and translator of Dante into Hungarian, died of throat cancer. From 1916 to his death he edited *Nyugat*, Hungary's most prestigious literary review. After a short phase of defiance occasioned by a negative review from the older poet, Radnóti came to admire Babits, whose staunch Catholicism and broad view of culture were a shield against the onslaught of Fascist barbarism. His name is pronounced '*Mee*-hai *Baa*-bich'.

'Spring Flies'
On 15 March 1942 an anti-war demonstration took place by the statue of the revolutionary poet Sándor Petőfi (1823–49). This poem was written shortly afterwards.
   the angel of past freedom: This phrase stands for national resistance to German imperialism and native Fascism.

'Fourth Eclogue'
When I was still unborn, if you'd only asked: Throughout his life Radnóti was haunted by the knowledge that his birth had cost the lives of both his mother and his twin brother. 'The Terrible Angel', p.63, deals with the same problem. See Introduction pp.13 and 15.

'Fifth Eclogue'
György Bálint, a left-wing journalist and a friend of Radnóti's, was sent to the Ukraine in a forced labour battalion. He was listed as 'missing' in 1943.

'I Cannot Tell'
Vörösmarty: (pronounced *Vuh*-rush-mar-tee). Mihály Vörösmarty (1800–55) was one of Hungary's major Romantic poets. He lived in a small Transdanubian village for part of his life.

'Oh Ancient Prisons'
Written a few days after the German occupation of Hungary, 19 March 1944. Admiral Horthy remained as a figurehead 'Regent', but the new administration gave unconditional support to the German war aims. In May 1944 the deportation of Hungarian Jews to Auschwitz began.

'Seventh Eclogue'
Written in the prison camp near the copper mines at Bor in Serbia. Although Radnóti wrote 'Lager Heideman' at the foot of this and other poems, he appears to have been mistaken, the correct name being Lager Heidenau.
   without putting in the accents: In Hungarian the length of a vowel is indicated by a diacritical mark over the vowel letter.

'A la Recherche'
there was a place they went to: i.e. Spain during the Civil War.

'Eighth Eclogue'
Written shortly before German troops evacuated the camps at Bor. The situation is desperate, but the end of the war and the hope of

liberation are now in sight. Some of the Prophet's lines are taken more or less verbatim from the Bible, in particular from the books of Nahum, Habakkuk and Isaiah.

'Postcards'
The original title is *Razglednicák* (picture postcards), a Serbian word with a Hungarian plural ending. The poems follow the forced march of the labour battalion from Serbia through Hungary towards Germany. During the march, friends and comrades of Radnóti's were shot dead by soldiers of a retreating German SS division. By the time they reached Győr in Western Hungary, Radnóti was unable to continue the march. The Hungarian soldiers escorting the unit tried to lodge those labourers who were weak or infirm in a hospital but, when this proved impossible, they led them to a small grove near the village of Abda and shot them. The last of these 'Postcards' was written nine days before the poet's death.

Der springt noch auf: 'That one can still get up': according to one account, a comment heard by Radnóti on the march when an S.S. soldier summarily executed one of his friends, the violinist Miklós Lovsi. In the event, Radnóti was killed, not by the Germans, but by Hungarian guards assigned to his unit.

Select Bibliography of Radnóti in English

TRANSLATIONS

Clouded Sky. Poems. Tr. Steven Polgar, Stephen Berg, S. J. Marks (New York, etc: Harper and Row, 1972).

Subway Stops. Poems. Tr. Emery George (Ann Arbor: Ardis, 1977).

The Witness: Selected Poems. Tr. Thomas Ország-Land (Market Drayton: Tern Press, 1977).

Forced March: Selected Poems. Tr. Clive Wilmer and George Gömöri (Manchester: Carcanet Press, 1979).

The Complete Poetry. Tr. Emery George (Ann Arbor: Ardis, 1980).

Under Gemini: A Diary about Childhood. Prose memoir and selected poetry. Tr. Kenneth M. and Zita McRobbie and Jascha Kessler (Budapest: Corvina/ Athens, Ohio: Ohio University Press, 1985).

33 Poems/ 33 vers. Bilingual selection. Tr. Thomas Ország-Land (Budapest: Maecenas, 1992).

Foamy Sky: The Major Poems of Miklós Radnóti. Tr. Zsuzsanna Ozsváth and Frederick Turner (Princeton: Princeton University Press, 1992).

The Last Poems of Miklós Radnóti. Tr. Peter Zollman (Privately published, n.d.[1994]).

Camp Notebook. Tr. Francis Jones (Todmorden: Arc, 2000).

SELECTED SECONDARY LITERATURE

Marianna D. Birnbaum, *Miklós Radnóti: A Biography of his Poetry* (Munich, 1983).

Emery George, *The Poetry of Miklós Radnóti: A Comparative Study* (New York, 1986).

George Gömöri and Clive Wilmer (eds.), *The Life and Poetry of Miklós Radnóti* (Boulder, Colorado, 1999).

Zsuzsanna Ozsváth, *In the Footsteps of Orpheus: The Life and Times of Miklós Radnóti* (Bloomington, Indiana, 2000).

BIOGRAPHIES

MIKLÓS RADNÓTI, one of the giants of modern Hungarian poetry, was born in Budapest in 1909. He was of Jewish extraction. Orphaned early in life, he knew little emotional security till his 1935 marriage to Fanni Gyarmati, the muse of his poems. His first book of poetry, *A Pagan Welcome*, was published in 1930, when he was 21. It consists of celebrations of life and love, naïve, formless and *avant-garde* in manner. Later volumes show the influence, first, of libertarian Socialism and, then, of Roman Catholicism. Radnóti's real talent does not emerge, however, till his fifth book, *Keep Walking, You, the Death-Condemned* (1936), where it is focused by his rising anxiety at the rise of fascism. This book and *Steep Path* (1938) reveal his growing preoccupation with fate and the deaths of poets in their youth. The latter also includes the first two of his Eclogues in classical metres. From 1940 on, with Hungary in the shadow of the Third Reich, Radnóti, like many others of Jewish race, was obliged to serve in forced labour battalions. The last of these – at Bor in Serbia – was evacuated in 1944 as the Germans retreated from the eastern front. Radnóti and his fellow labourers were force-marched back into Hungary, where on 9 November, too weak to carry on, he and many comrades were executed by firing-squad. The following year the bodies were exhumed. Radnóti's was identified by a notebook of poems in his greatcoat pocket. These were published in 1946 under the title *Foaming Sky*.

GEORGE (GYÖRGY) GÖMÖRI was born in Budapest. After taking part in the 1956 revolution, he fled to England and studied at Oxford. From 1969 to 2001 he taught Polish and Hungarian Literature at Cambridge University. His books include a monograph on the Polish poet Cyprian Norwid and a book of essays on modern Polish literature, *Magnetic Poles* (The Polish Cultural Foundation, 2000). As well as producing eight books of poetry in Hungarian, he has co-edited with George Szirtes an anthology of modern Hungarian poetry, *The Colonnade of Teeth* (Bloodaxe, 1996). He was awarded the Salvatore Quasimodo Prize in 1993 and the Ada Negri Poetry Prize in 1995.

CLIVE WILMER was born in 1945, grew up in London and studied at Cambridge University, where he still teaches. He has had four poetry collections published by Carcanet Press and a fifth collection, *The Falls* (2001), by the Worple Press. A freelance writer and lecturer, he has edited prose work by Thom Gunn and Donald Davie and anthologised the writings of John Ruskin, William Morris and D. G. Rossetti. In 1998 he was awarded The Endre Ady Memorial Medal for Translation by the Hungarian PEN Club, and a selection of his work, *The Infinite Variety*, has been translated into Hungarian by George Gömöri and Anna T. Szabó (Szeged: JATE Press, 2002).

As well as collaborating on translations of Radnóti's work, Clive Wilmer and George Gömöri have co-translated two collections of György Petri, the second of which, *Eternal Monday*, was shortlisted for the Weidenfeld Translation Prize in 2001.